GRADE 2

AGES 7-8

Subtraction

Learning Fun Workbook

Published by Highlights Learning • 815 Church Street • Honesdale, Pennsylvania 18431
ISBN: 978-1-68437-931-6
Mfg. 10/2019
Printed in Guangzhou, Guangdong, China
First edition
10 9 8 7 6 5 4 3 2 1

For assistance in the preparation of this book, the editors would like to thank:
Kristin Ward, K–5 Mathematics and Science Instructional Coach; MS Curriculum, Instruction, and Assessment
Jump Start Press, Inc.

Count Down!

When you count backward, you do not say the start number.

5, 4, 3, 2, 1 . . . blast off! You can count back to subtract. Here's how.

The start number is 10. 10 − 3 = ☐

Count back 3. 9 8 7

The last number is your answer. 10 − 3 = 7

Fill in the missing numbers to count back. Then fill in the answer to the subtraction equation.

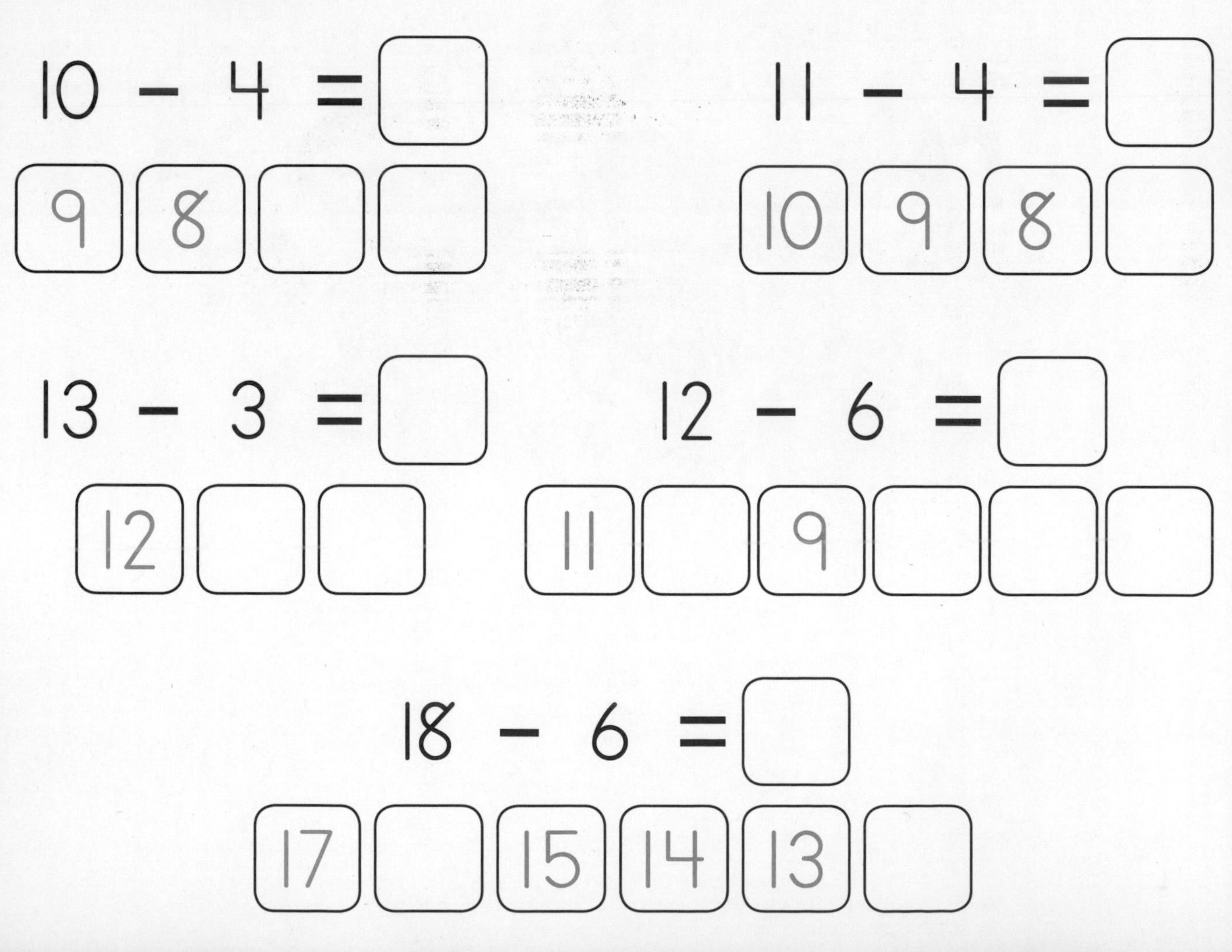

Count back to solve these subtraction problems.

$7 - 4 = \square$ $16 - 3 = \square$

$17 - 2 = \square$ $9 - 3 = \square$

$8 - 2 = \square$ $11 - 5 = \square$

What silly things do you see at space camp?

Robot Parts

Related facts use the same numbers. When the facts are related, they all work in the same bar model or number bond.

Taking apart a whole is one way to think about subtraction. You can use a number bond or bar model to take apart a problem. Both show how 2 parts (smaller numbers) make up a whole (larger number). More than one pair of numbers might work with the same larger number. Here's what that might look like.

Robin has **14** robot parts. Some are long and some are short. How many of each could she have?

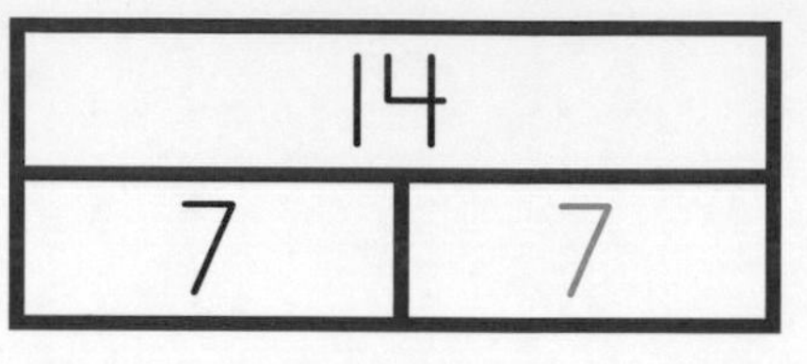

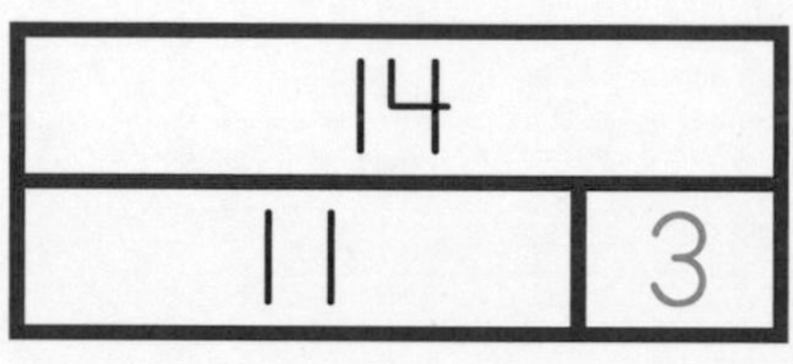

Take apart a subtraction problem using a **number bond**. Then solve the problem. We did one to get you started.

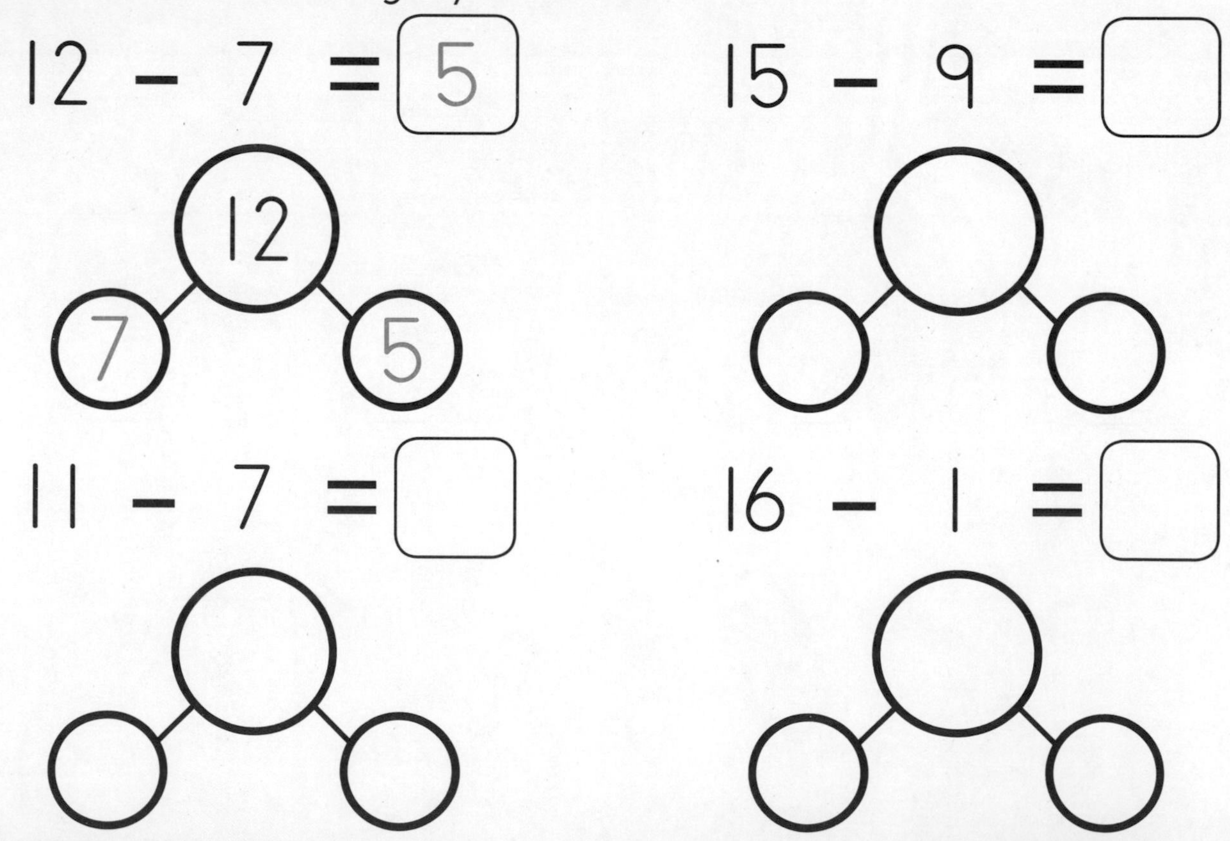

Take apart each subtraction problem using a **bar model**. Then solve the problem. We did one to get you started.

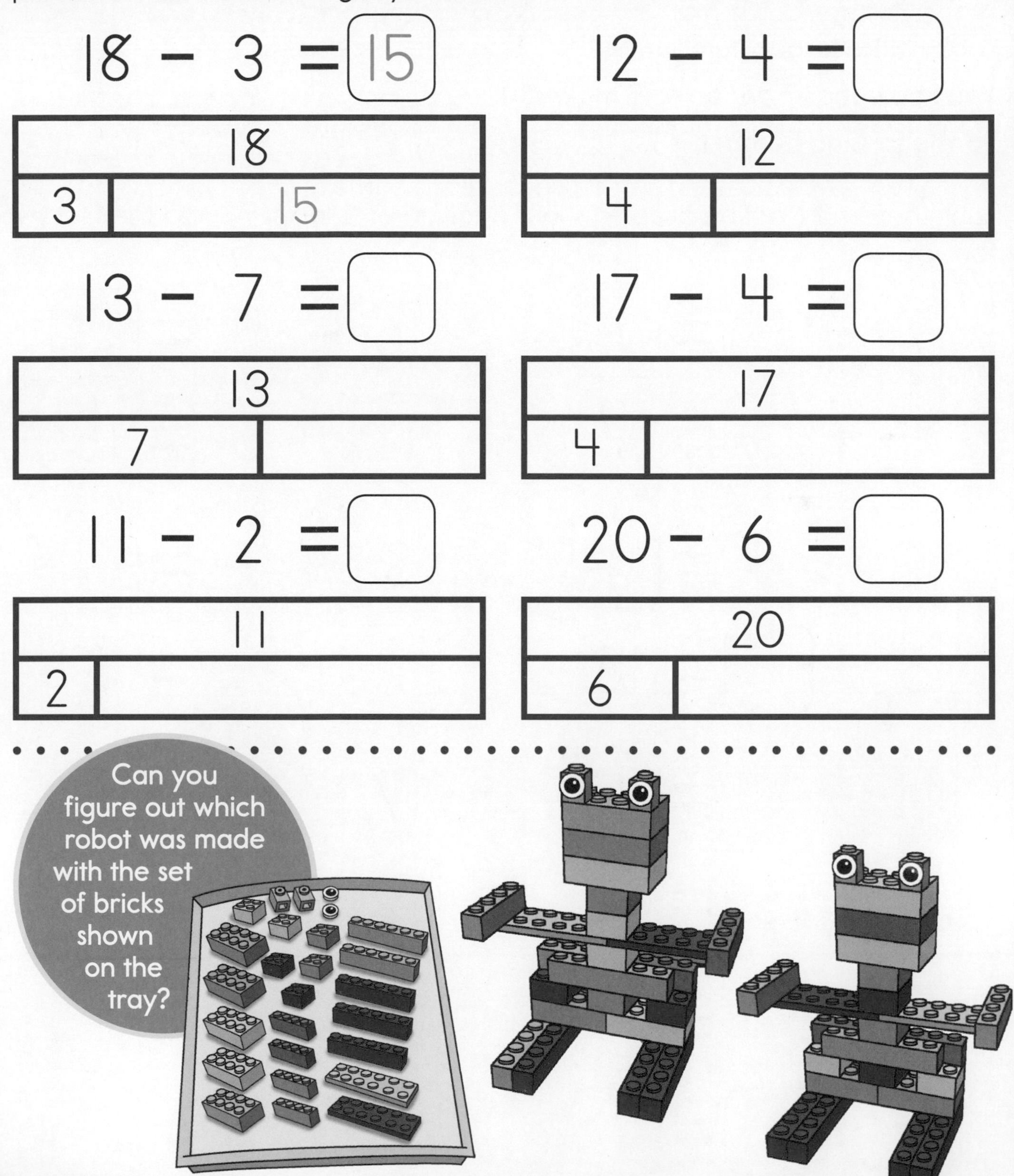

All in the Family

10, 7, and 3 are part of a fact family.

You can use addition to help you subtract.

10 − 3 = ?

Look at the larger number.

You know that 7 added to 3 makes 10.

So the missing number is 7.

3 + 7 = 10

10 − 3 = 7

Turn these subtraction problems into addition problems. We did the first two for you.

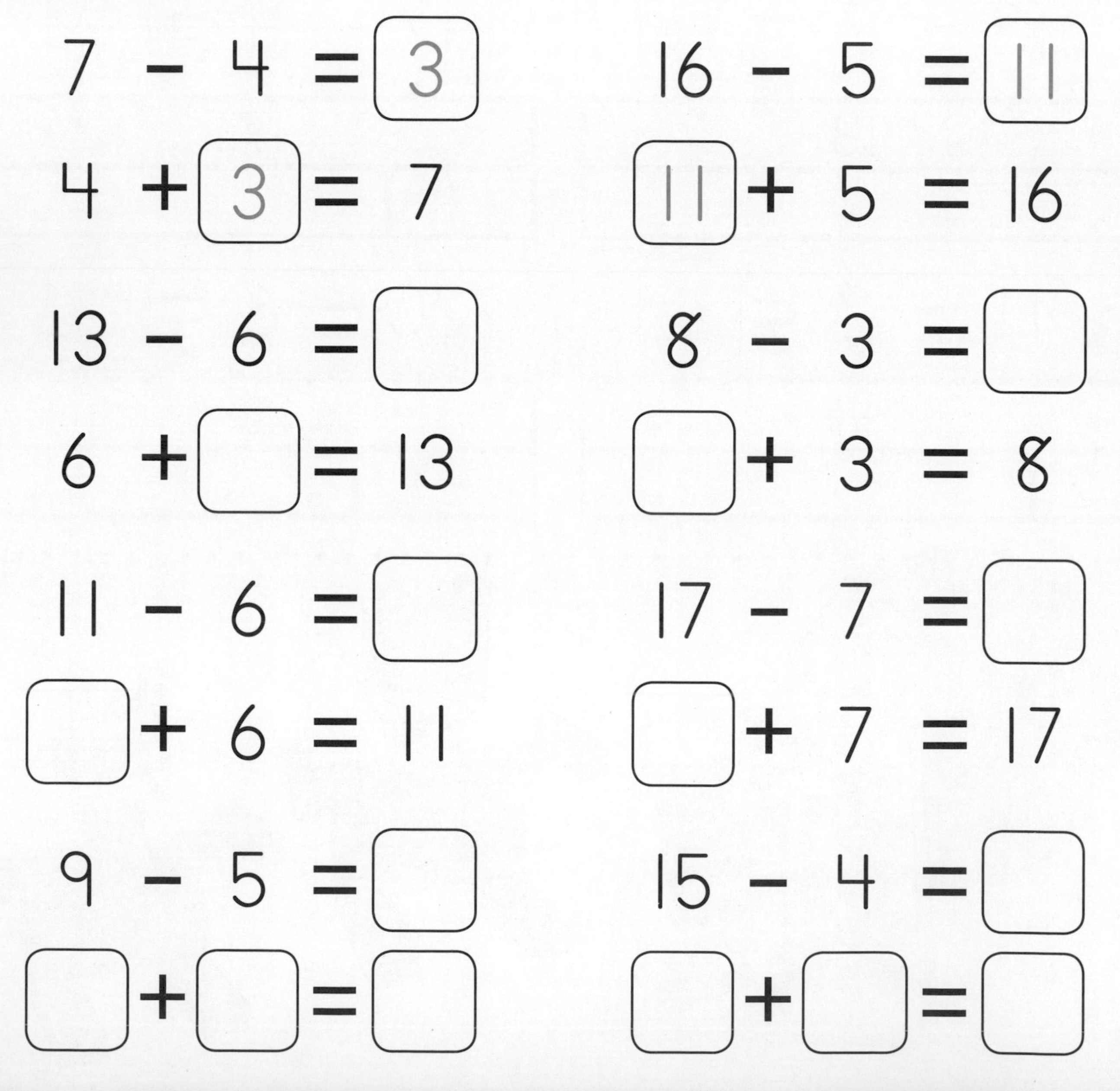

Write the equation to show the fact family. Then solve the subtraction problem.

$16 - 9 = \square$

$\square + \square = \square$

$12 - 5 = \square$

$\square + \square = \square$

$14 - 4 = \square$

$\square + \square = \square$

$19 - 8 = \square$

$\square + \square = \square$

Find and color the **10** objects in this Hidden Pictures puzzle. Then color the rest of the picture.

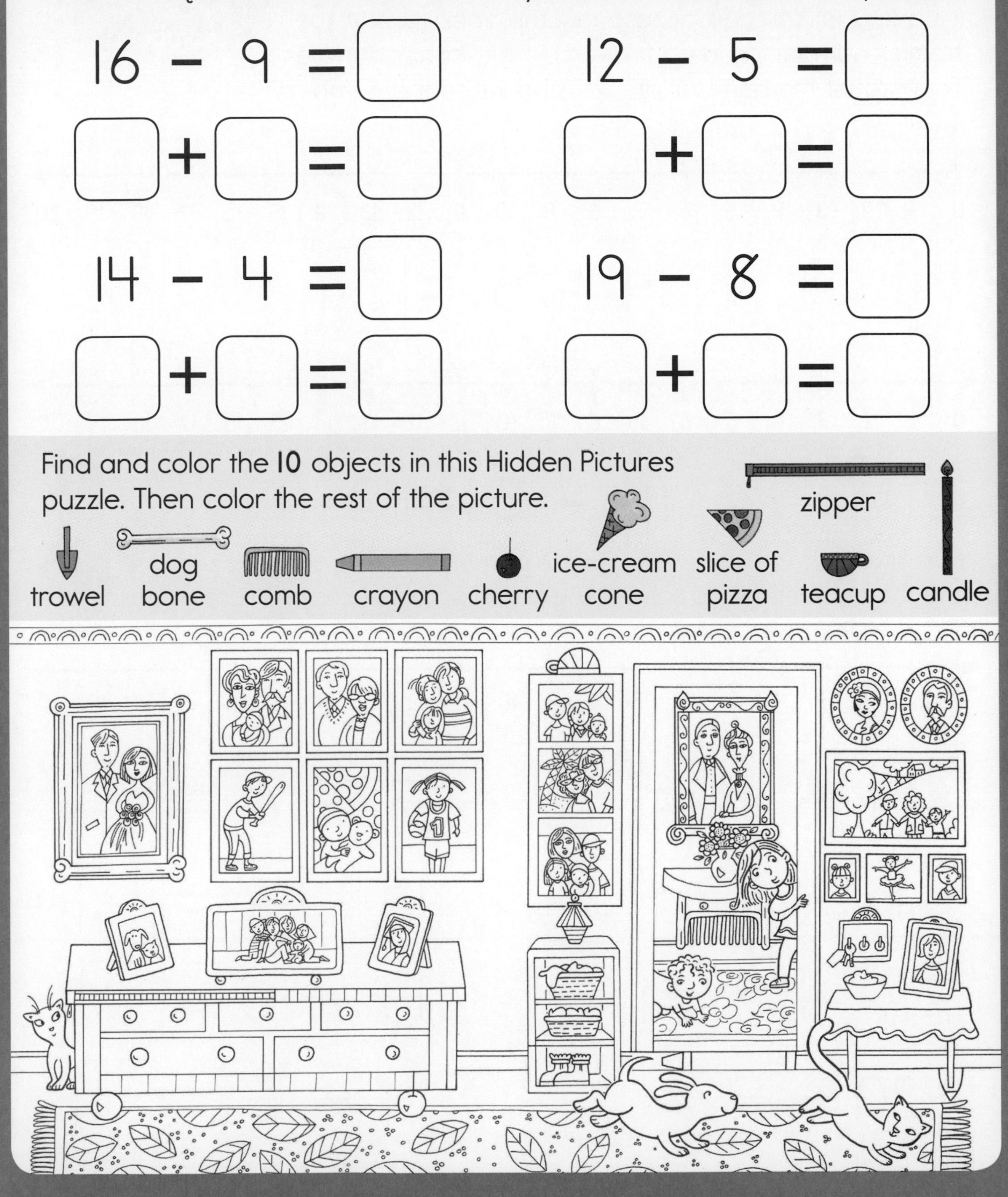

Jump on It!

When you subtract using a number line, you are finding the distance between 2 numbers.

You can use a number line to subtract. How you do it is up to you! You can choose to jump backward to the smaller number or jump forward to the larger number. Then count the number of jumps between the numbers.

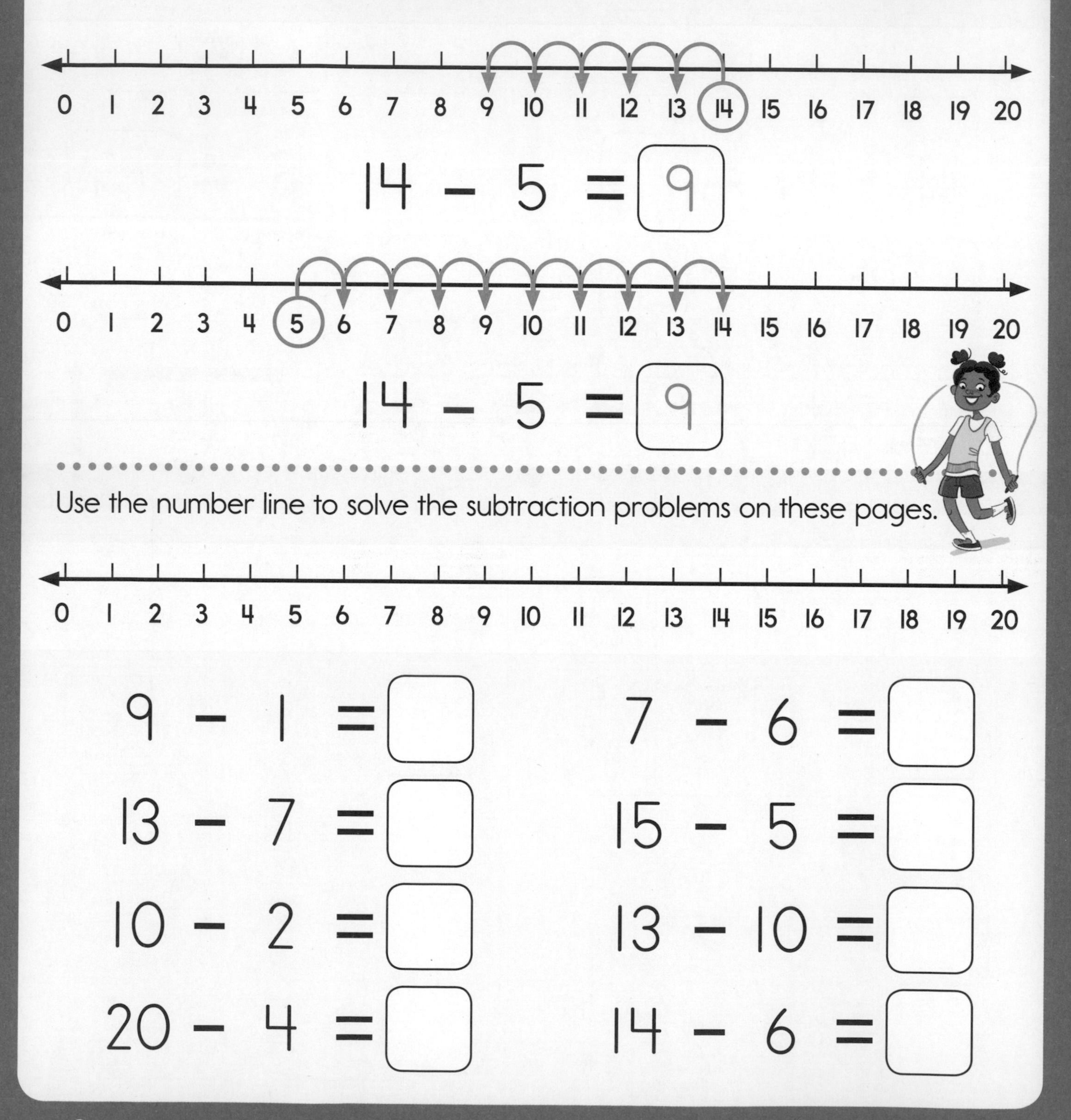

Use the number line to solve the subtraction problems on these pages.

9 - 1 = ☐

7 - 6 = ☐

13 - 7 = ☐

15 - 5 = ☐

10 - 2 = ☐

13 - 10 = ☐

20 - 4 = ☐

14 - 6 = ☐

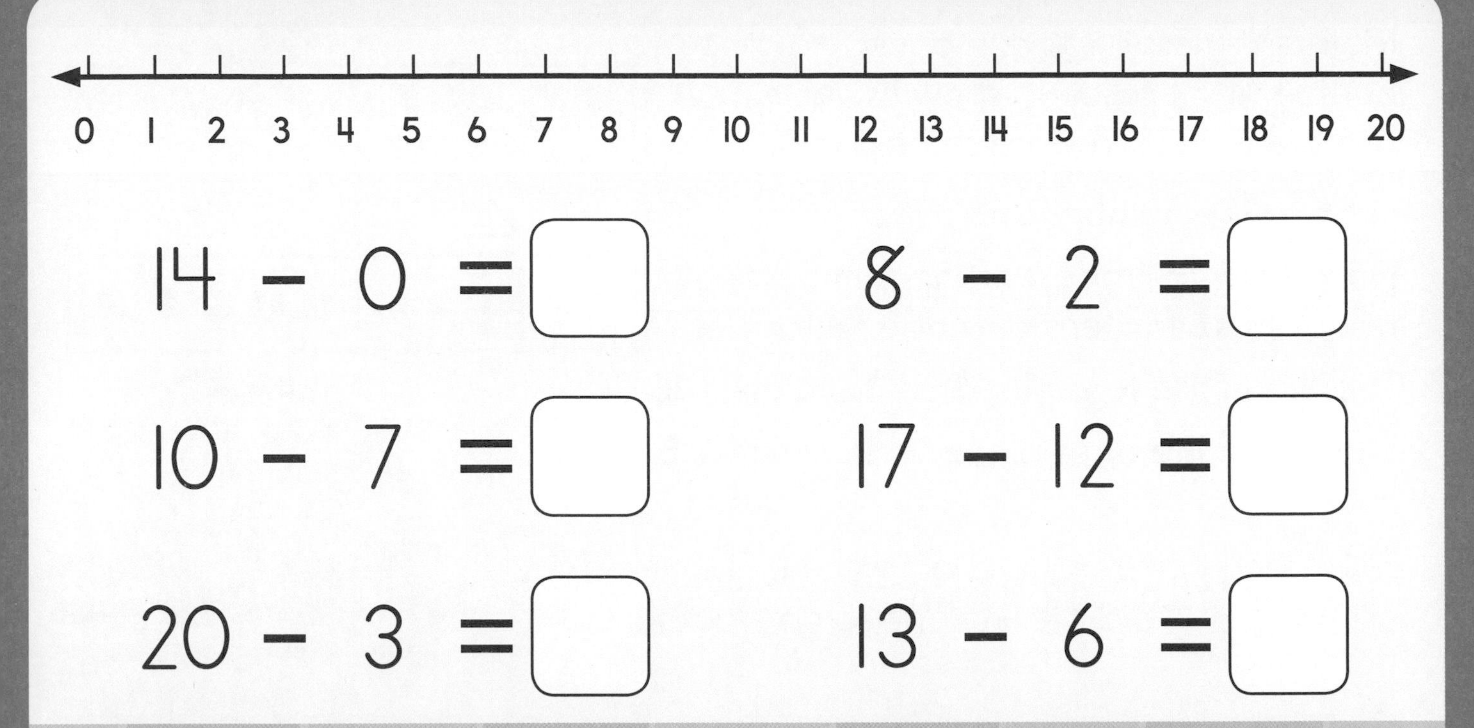

$14 - 0 = \square$ $8 - 2 = \square$

$10 - 7 = \square$ $17 - 12 = \square$

$20 - 3 = \square$ $13 - 6 = \square$

Help these jump ropers find their partners. Follow each rope to see who is partnered with whom.

In Its Place

Knowing place value can help you subtract.

Math isn't messy! You can put a two-digit number in its place to show its value. Use **base-ten drawings** to help you.

Look at the number 25.

Now draw to represent the numbers using lines I for tens and dots ● for ones.

Tens	Ones
2	5
I I	● ● ● ● ●

The 2 is in the tens place, so its value is 20.

The 5 is in the ones place, so its value is 5.

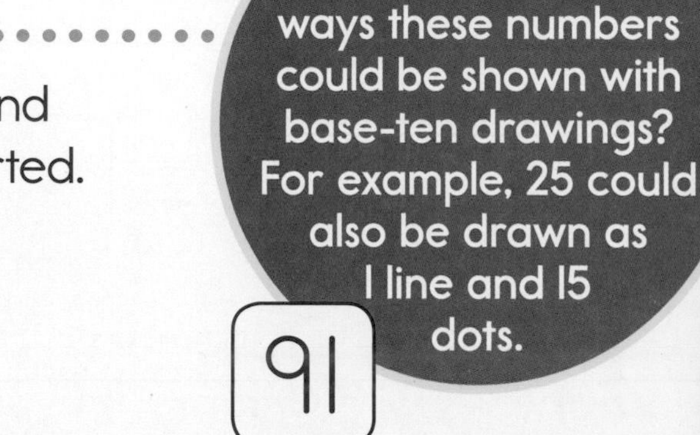

Fill in each place-value chart with numbers and drawings. We did the first one to get you started.

Tens	Ones
3	7
I I I	● ● ● ● ● ● ●

91

Tens	Ones

Tens	Ones

Tens	Ones

Now use place value for three-digit numbers. Fill in each place-value chart with numbers and drawings. Use squares ■ for hundreds. We did the first one for you.

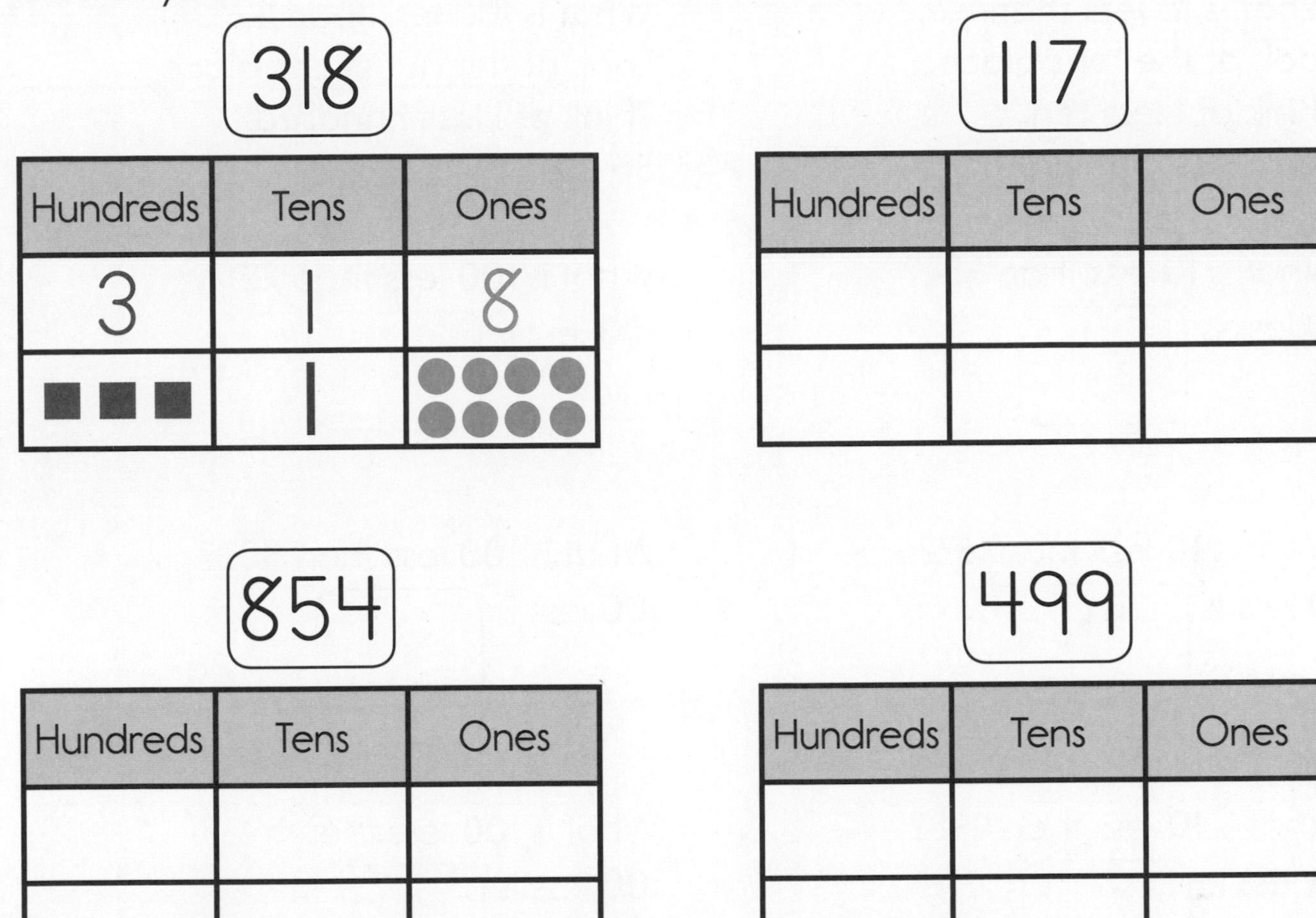

318

Hundreds	Tens	Ones
3	1	8
■■■	|	●●●●●●●●

117

Hundreds	Tens	Ones

854

Hundreds	Tens	Ones

499

Hundreds	Tens	Ones

Three friends entered their frogs in a jumping contest. Use the clues to figure out whose frog is whose, and which frog came in which place.

Clues:

1. Lucas's frog finished after Leapy.
2. Logan's frog, Leapy, finished before Leah's frog and Lily.
3. Larry finished second.

Use the chart to keep track of your answers. Put an **X** in each box that can't be true and an **O** in boxes that are true.

	Larry	Lily	Leapy	1st	2nd	3rd
Lucas						
Logan						
Leah						

Ten Less, Anyone?

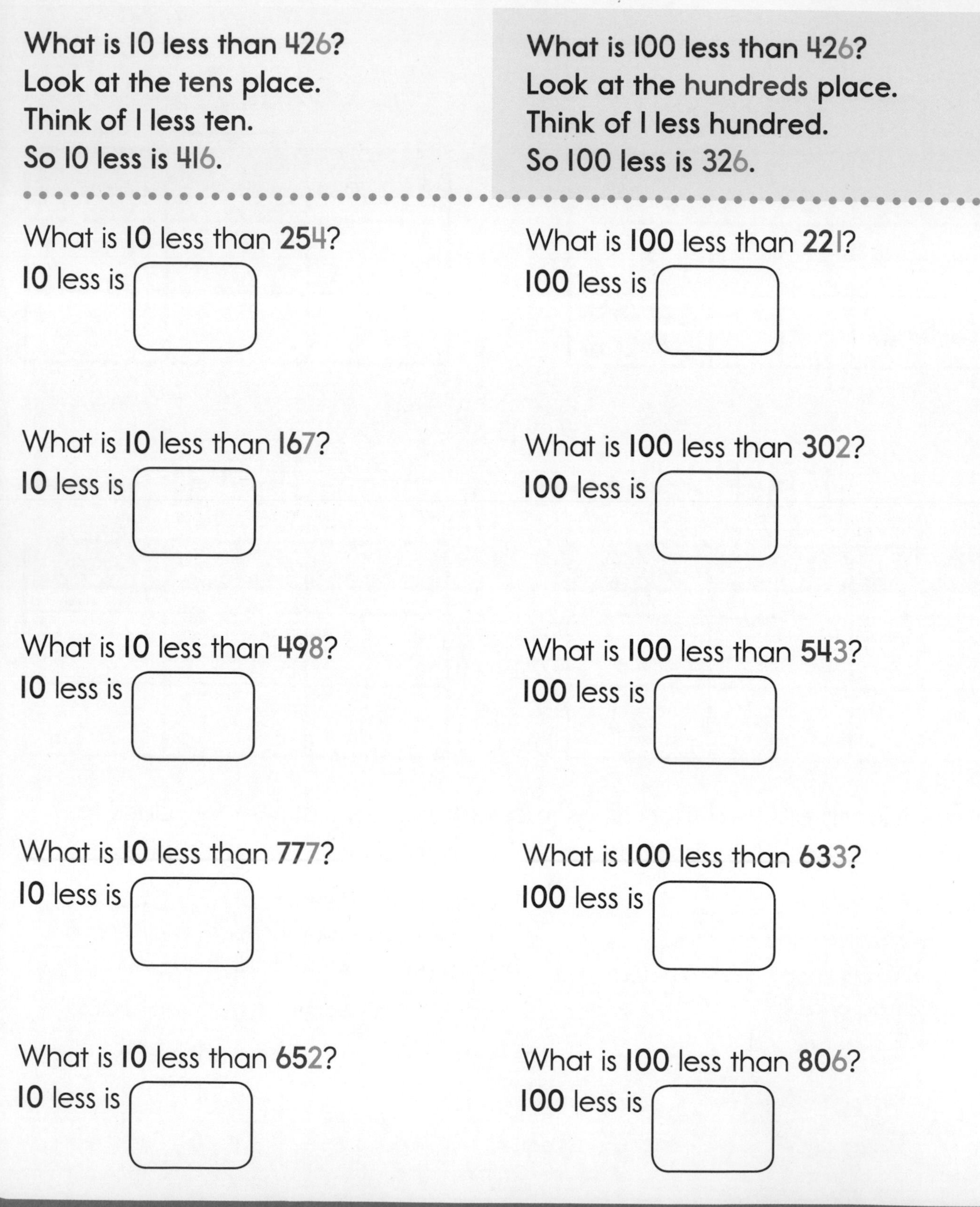

You can use mental math to subtract 10 or 100. See how quickly you can fetch the answer! Here's how.

What is 10 less than 426?
Look at the tens place.
Think of 1 less ten.
So 10 less is 416.

What is 100 less than 426?
Look at the hundreds place.
Think of 1 less hundred.
So 100 less is 326.

What is **10** less than **254**?
10 less is

What is **10** less than **167**?
10 less is

What is **10** less than **498**?
10 less is

What is **10** less than **777**?
10 less is

What is **10** less than **652**?
10 less is

What is **100** less than **221**?
100 less is

What is **100** less than **302**?
100 less is

What is **100** less than **543**?
100 less is

What is **100** less than **633**?
100 less is

What is **100** less than **806**?
100 less is

Help Rex fetch! To catch the tennis ball, Rex must run only along the path that is 10 less or 100 less than the last number he passed. Move up or down, left or right.

START

967	957	937	935	835	727
966	857	847	846	717	716
856	956	747	757	617	517
756	867	647	637	627	417
727	757	747	537	527	427
627	527	447	427	407	327

FINISH

What's Next?

Numbers can follow a pattern that will help you to subtract. You can look at the place value to find number patterns. Then you can figure out what number comes next. Here's how.

Look at the tens place. 250, 240, 230, ?
The tens numbers are going down.
Fill in the next number. 250, 240, 230, 220

Look at the hundreds place. 626, 526, 426, ?
The hundreds numbers are going down.
Fill in the next number. 626, 526, 426, 326

Use place value and number patterns to fill in each missing number on this quilt.

Can you spot **15** differences between these quilt patterns?

Cross It Off!

You can use a hundred chart to subtract two-digit numbers. Knowing the place value of tens helps, too. Here's how.

54 – 32 = ?

Start on 54.

To subtract 32, move up 3 rows to count back 3 tens.

Then move left 2 boxes to count back 2 ones.

Where you end up gives you the answer.

54 – 32 = 22

1	2	3	4	5	6	7	8	9	10
11	12	13	14	15	16	17	18	19	20
21	22	23	24	25	26	27	28	29	30
31	32	33	34	35	36	37	38	39	40
41	42	43	44	45	46	47	48	49	50
51	52	53	54	55	56	57	58	59	60
61	62	63	64	65	66	67	68	69	70
71	72	73	74	75	76	77	78	79	80
81	82	83	84	85	86	87	88	89	90
91	92	93	94	95	96	97	98	99	100

Solve each problem on these 2 pages using the hundred chart. Then use your answers to solve the riddle on the next page.

33 – 12 = ☐

87 – 33 = ☐

49 – 15 = ☐

77 – 16 = ☐

25 – 14 = ☐

68 – 22 = ☐

93 – 21 = ☐

55 – 43 = ☐

$74 - 23 = \square$

$59 - 42 = \square$

$57 - 37 = \square$

$96 - 51 = \square$

$100 - 33 = \square$

$68 - 26 = \square$

$88 - 14 = \square$

$77 - 44 = \square$

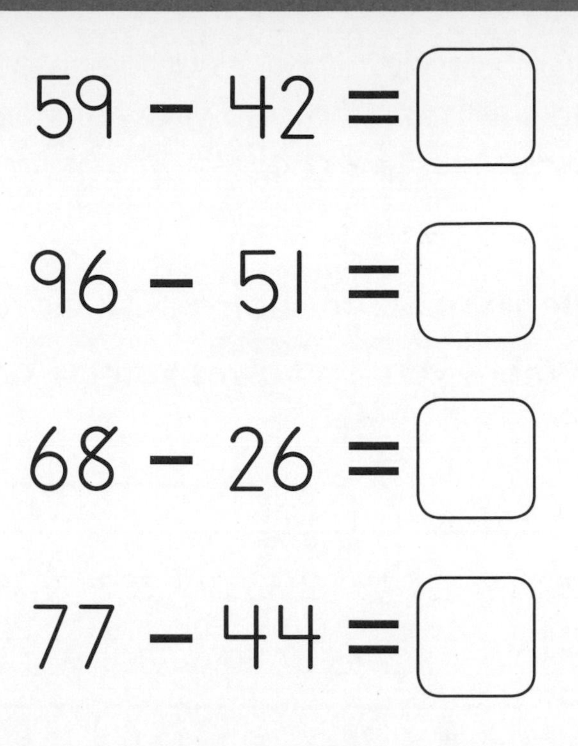

Cross out the boxes that hold numbers that match your answers. When you're done, write the remaining letters in order from left to right and top to bottom. They will give you the answer to the riddle.

What do creatures in fairy tales learn in school?

T 44	T 20	M 61	H 92	A 45
R 74	E 29	E 21	E 64	A 54
L 10	I 67	T 72	M 34	F 36
R 51	F 17	A 83	Y 46	B 57
E 71	J 42	K 12	T 57	H 11

___ ___ ___ ___ ___ ___ ___-___ ___ ___ ___

Hang On!

Remember you are finding the distance between 2 numbers. You can start at either number.

You can zip along a number line in either direction to subtract. Knowing your tens place value can make it easier. Here's how.

52 – 23 = ?

Begin at 52. To subtract 23, move left 2 tens. Move left 3 ones.

Where you land gives you the answer.

52 – 23 = 29

25 26 27 28 29 30 31 32 33 34 35 36 37 38 39 40 41 42 43 44 45 46 47 48 49 50 51 52 53 54 55

You get the same answer if you start at **23** and jump to **52**!

22 23 24 25 26 27 28 29 30 31 32 33 34 35 36 37 38 39 40 41 42 43 44 45 46 47 48 49 50 51 52

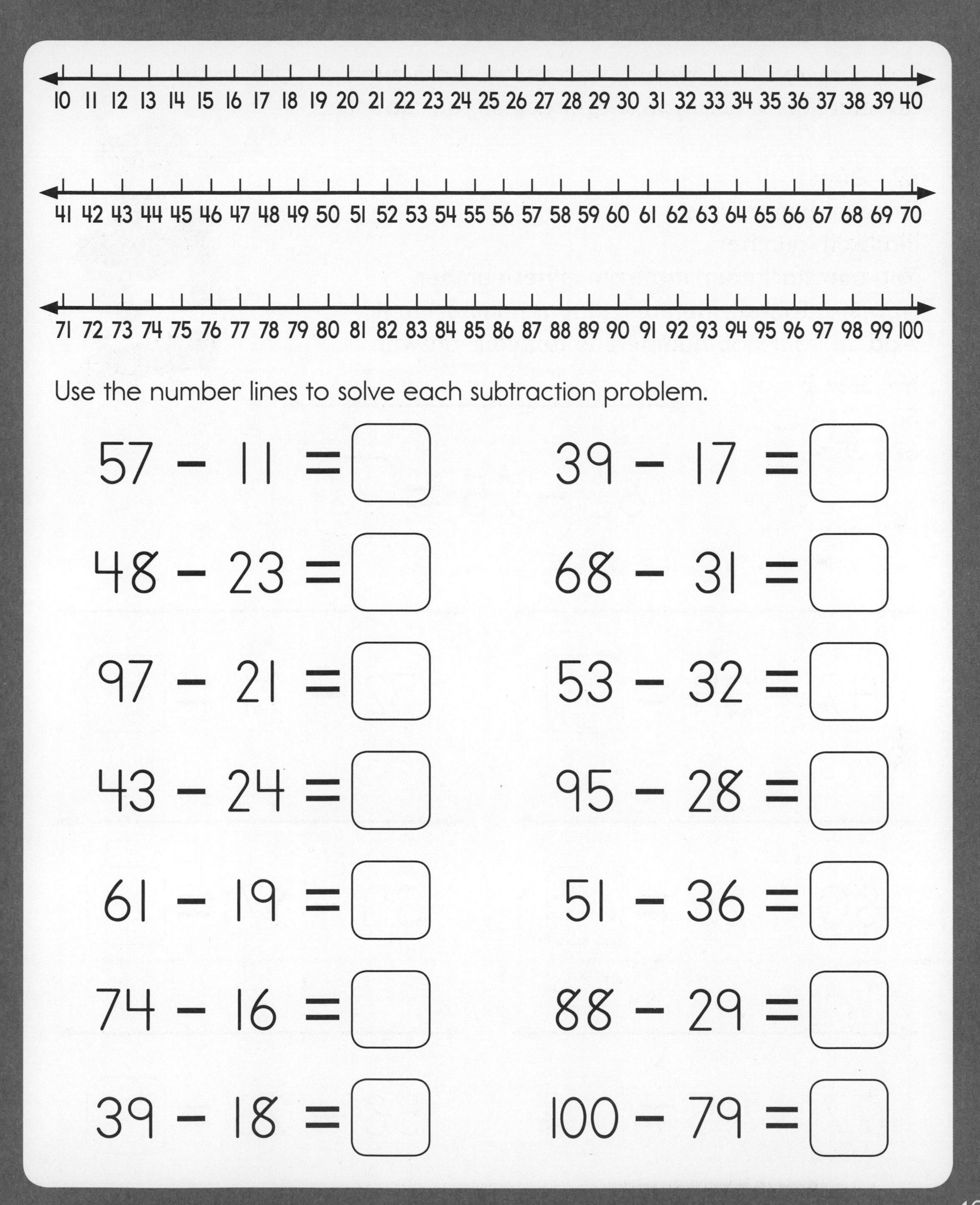

Use the number lines to solve each subtraction problem.

57 − 11 = ☐

39 − 17 = ☐

48 − 23 = ☐

68 − 31 = ☐

97 − 21 = ☐

53 − 32 = ☐

43 − 24 = ☐

95 − 28 = ☐

61 − 19 = ☐

51 − 36 = ☐

74 − 16 = ☐

88 − 29 = ☐

39 − 18 = ☐

100 − 79 = ☐

Ramp Up

Count by tens and ones to subtract two-digit numbers. Use an open number line to help you keep track of your counting.

62 - 25 = ?
Draw a number line.
Plot both numbers.
You can start counting from either number.
Hop to a friendly number (a tens number) first.
Add up your hop numbers to get your answer.

5 + 30 + 2 = 37,
So . . .
62 - 25 = 37

5 30 2
25 30 60 62

62 - 25 = 37

47 - 34 =

52 - 11 =

80 - 26 =

39 - 17 =

77 - 45 =

58 - 23 =

$65 - 27 =$ ☐

$92 - 52 =$ ☐

$77 - 18 =$ ☐

$61 - 17 =$ ☐

Jump on in and see if you can spot **17** skateboards. Then look for **2** boards that match.

Tool Time

Which strategy worked best for which problems?

Now pick up the subtraction tools you have learned so far to solve these problems. Try using a hundred chart, a number line, mental math, or base-ten drawings.

75 − 50 = ☐

55 − 38 = ☐

21 − 11 = ☐

36 − 19 = ☐

38 − 27 = ☐

51 − 25 = ☐

78 − 35 = ☐

72 − 38 = ☐

1	2	3	4	5	6	7	8	9	10
11	12	13	14	15	16	17	18	19	20
21	22	23	24	25	26	27	28	29	30
31	32	33	34	35	36	37	38	39	40
41	42	43	44	45	46	47	48	49	50
51	52	53	54	55	56	57	58	59	60
61	62	63	64	65	66	67	68	69	70
71	72	73	74	75	76	77	78	79	80
81	82	83	84	85	86	87	88	89	90
91	92	93	94	95	96	97	98	99	100

63 − 48 = ☐

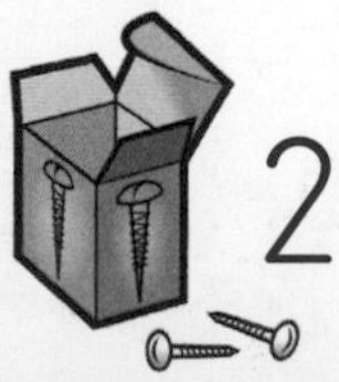

23 − 17 = ☐

$42 - 29 = \square$

$94 - 69 = \square$

$66 - 30 = \square$

$82 - 22 = \square$

$51 - 46 = \square$

$70 - 43 = \square$

$83 - 37 = \square$

$99 - 26 = \square$

Some tools and other items have been "subtracted" from this workshop. Can you find the **12** missing items? Draw them back in if you like.

Bits and Pieces

When you decompose a number, you break it down into smaller parts to get to a friendly ten number.

These numbers are going to pieces! **Decomposing** can help when subtracting from a two-digit number. Here's how it works.

Look at the ones in the two-digit number.

Then break apart the other number to include that ones number.

Subtract the ones. The answer will be a tens.

Subtract the remaining ones.

33 − 5 = ?

(5 → 3 and 2)

33 − 3 = 30

30 − 2 = 28

33 − 5 = 28

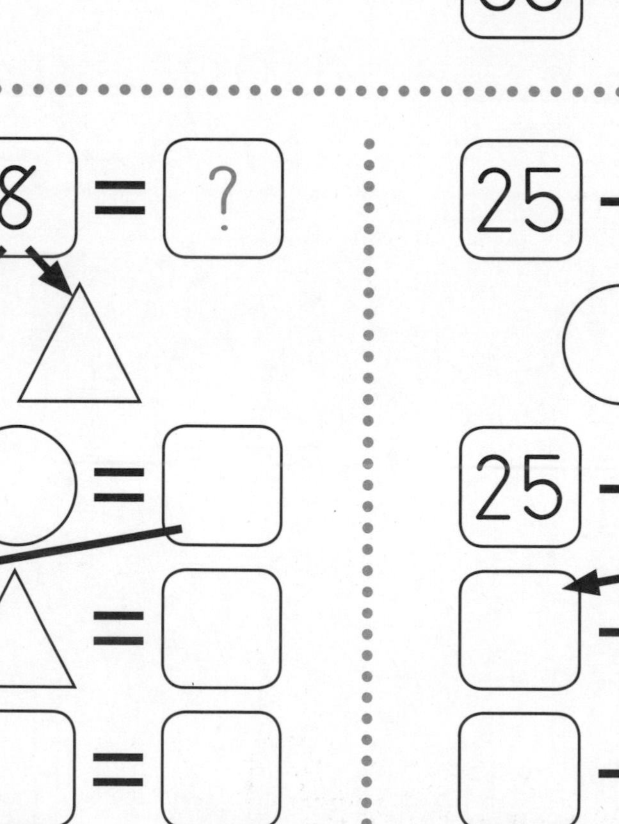

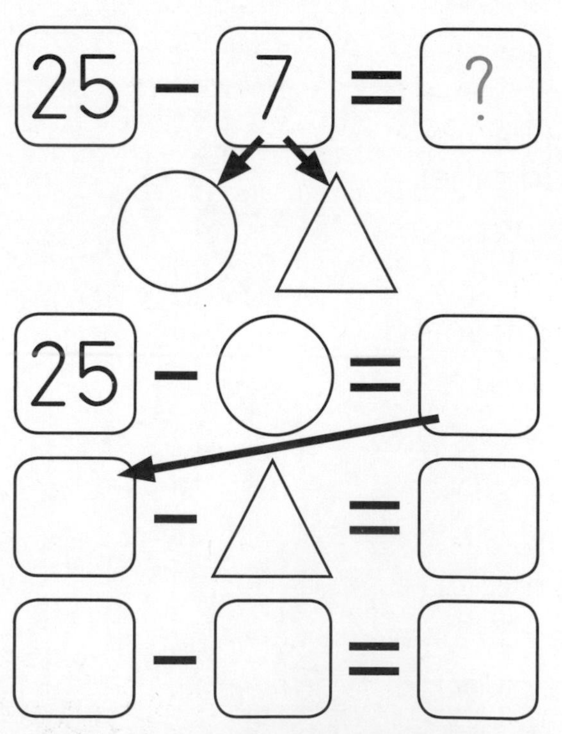

Solve these problems the same way. Remember to break down ones to make a ten.

$51 - 6 = \square$

$98 - 9 = \square$

$82 - 3 = \square$

$42 - 4 = \square$

Draw lines to match each tower to the set of blocks used to build it.

Break It Up!

When you decompose a number, you break it down into smaller parts to get to a friendly ten number.

Break apart, or **decompose**, two-digit numbers into tens and ones to help you subtract. Here's how.

45 - 23 = ?

Break the numbers into tens and ones.

Subtract the tens first.

Then subtract the ones.

Then add the 2 answers together.

So . . .

45 - 23 = 22

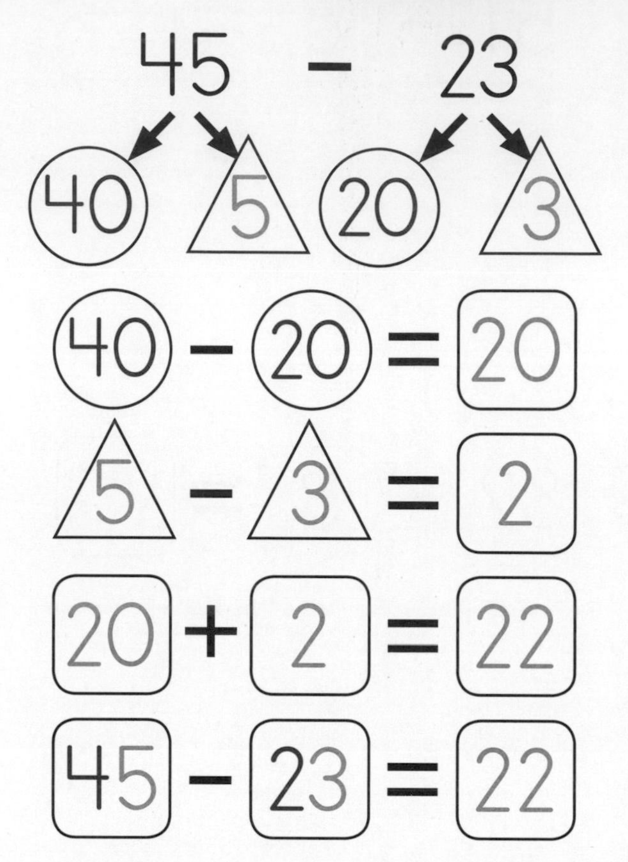

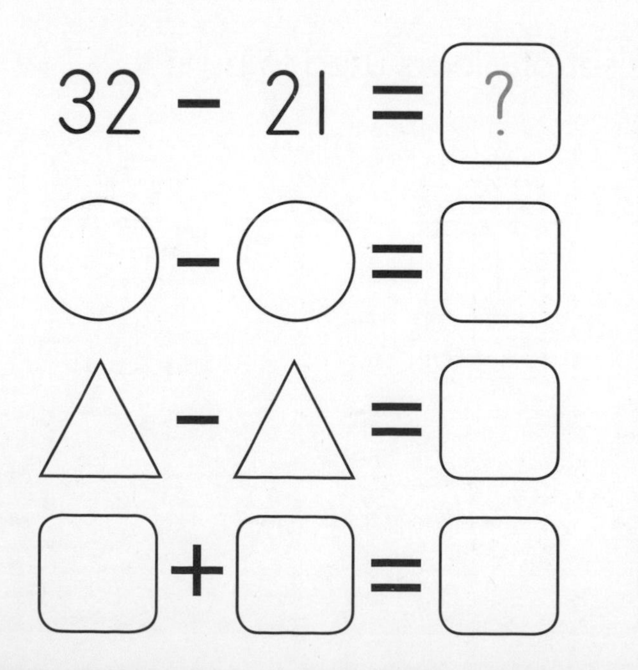

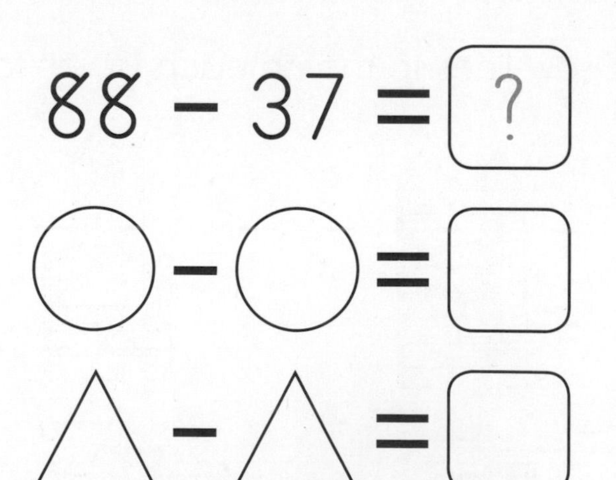

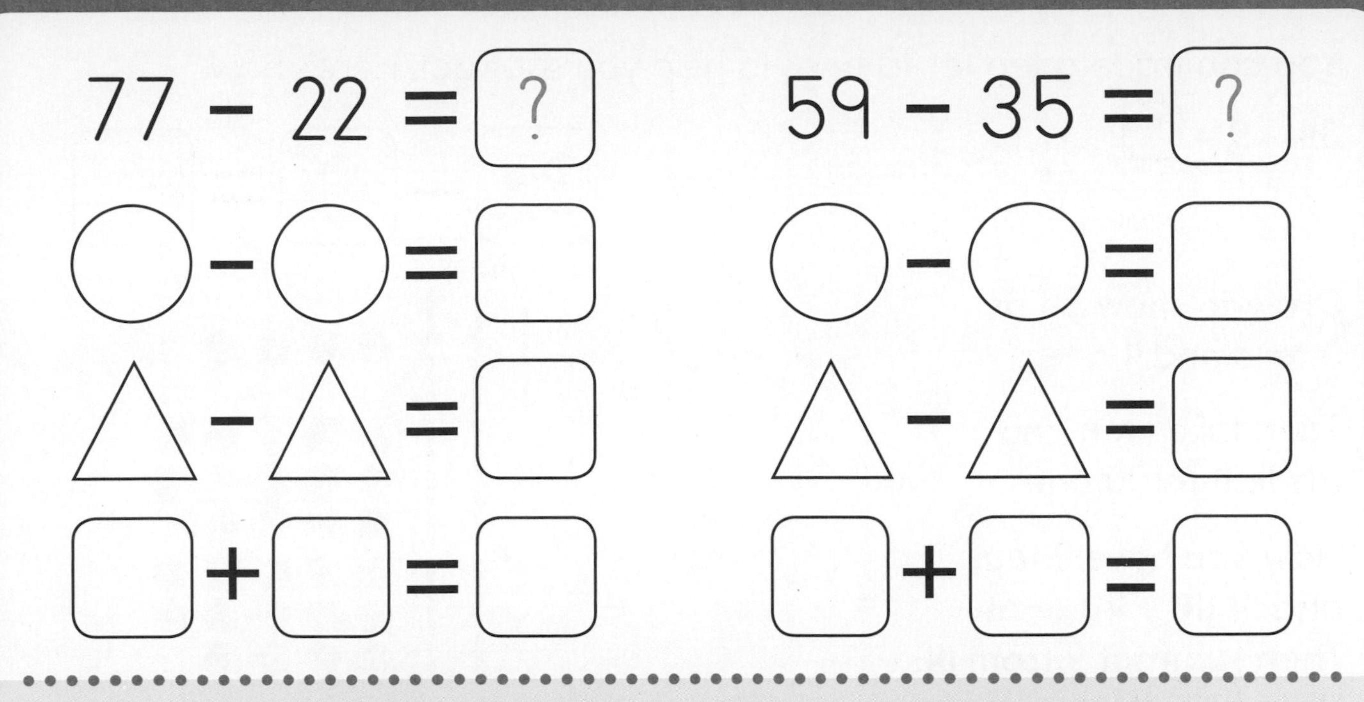

Which 3 pieces will finish the puzzle? Draw lines to place each piece.

Make a Trade!

You can trade a ten for 10 ones to help you subtract. Here's how.

34 – 9 = ?

34 – 9 = [ ]

tens ones

Draw to show 34 as
3 tens and 4 ones.

Then take 1 ten and
trade it for 10 ones.

Now you have 2 tens
and 14 (10 + 4) ones.
Then subtract 9 from 14.
How many tens and ones are left?

2 tens and 5 ones.

So . . .
34 – 9 = 25

34 + 9 = 25

Solve these subtraction problems by trading tens.

24 – 7 = [ ]

46 – 7 = [ ]

27 – 9 = [ ]

53 – 5 = [ ]

$43 - 8 = \square$

$96 - 7 = \square$

$62 - 5 = \square$

$53 - 7 = \square$

$41 - 9 = \square$

$92 - 6 = \square$

These friends got ready for Halloween in a hurry. Now their costumes are mixed up! Luckily, they're all wearing the right shoes. Figure out which costume pieces they should trade.

Fill 'Er Up!

A **place-value chart** can help you subtract a two-digit number. It can also help you fill up on ones if you run out. Here's how.

51 – 37 = ?

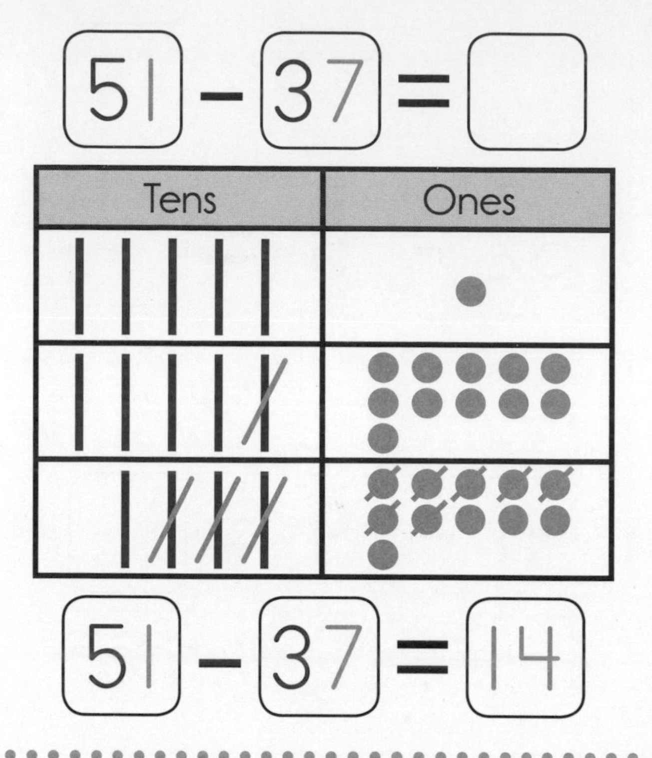

Record **51** in the place-value chart:
5 tens and **1** ones.
Next, trade **1** ten for **10** ones.
That leaves **1** less ten and
10 more ones.
Now you can subtract **37**,
or **3** tens and **7** ones.

So ...
51 – 37 = 14

Solve the subtraction problems on these 2 pages. Use the place-value charts to record your work.

36 – 17 = ☐

Tens	Ones

45 – 28 = ☐

Tens	Ones

$94 - 26 = \square$

Tens	Ones

$44 - 39 = \square$

Tens	Ones

See the Difference?

Solve these problems using any subtraction strategy. You can decompose numbers, draw pictures, use place values, or try other strategies. You can even make up your own strategies!

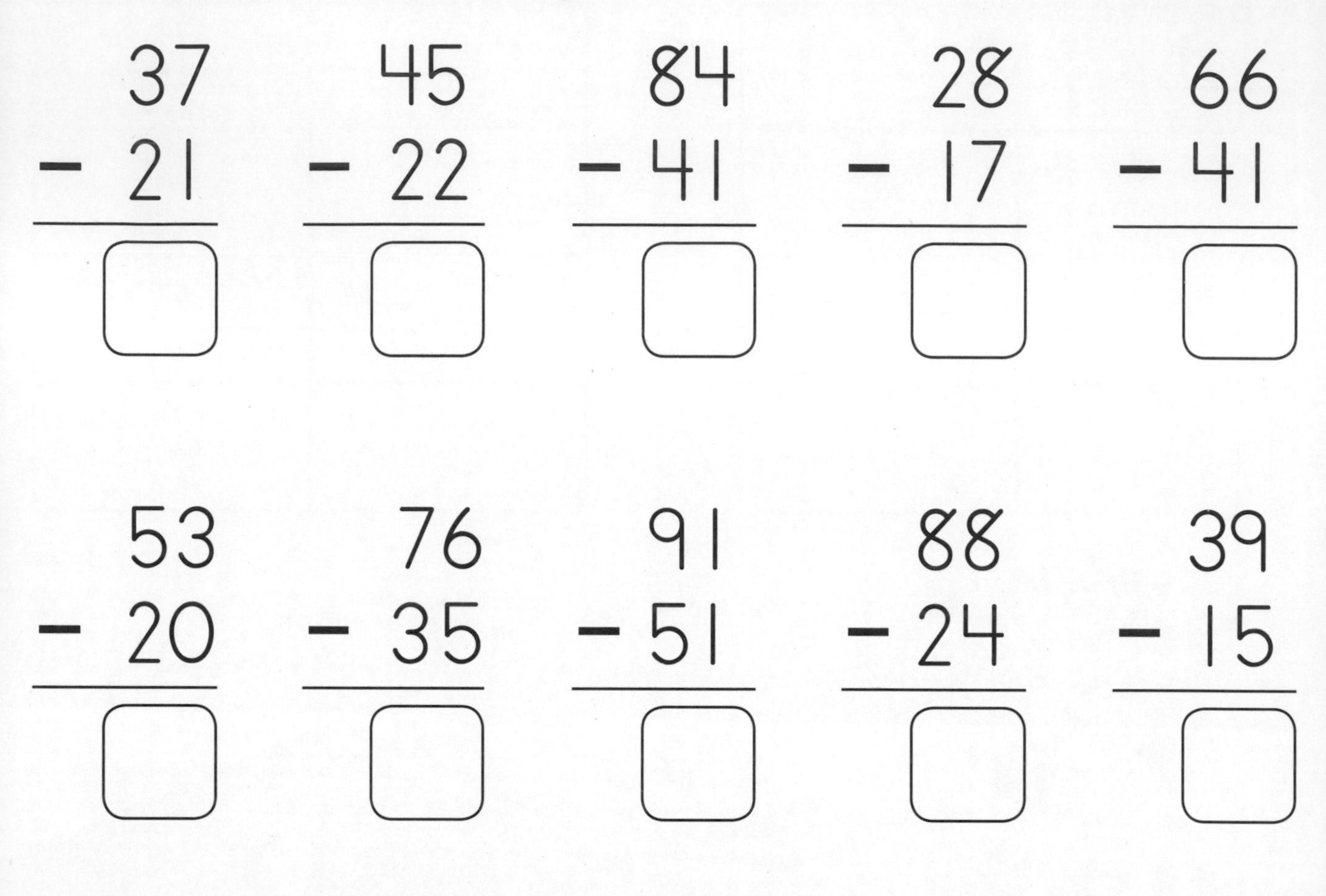

The answers to subtraction problems are called **differences**. Can you find 15 differences between the pictures below the subtraction problems?

Sub-Attractions!

Everyone is at the state fair today! Solve these word problems about what happened on the midway. You can use any of the subtraction strategies you've learned.

All **36** seats on the Cyclone roller coaster were filled. Then **7** people got off. How many people stayed for the next roller-coaster ride?

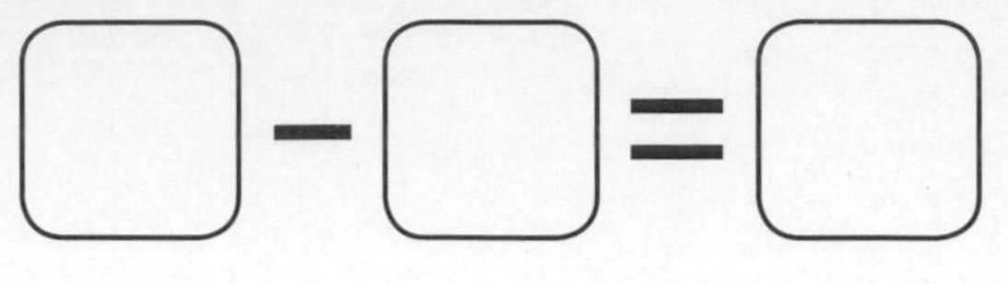

There were **42** stuffed rabbits to win at the Basketball Toss. By the end of the day **18** were left. How many rabbits were won?

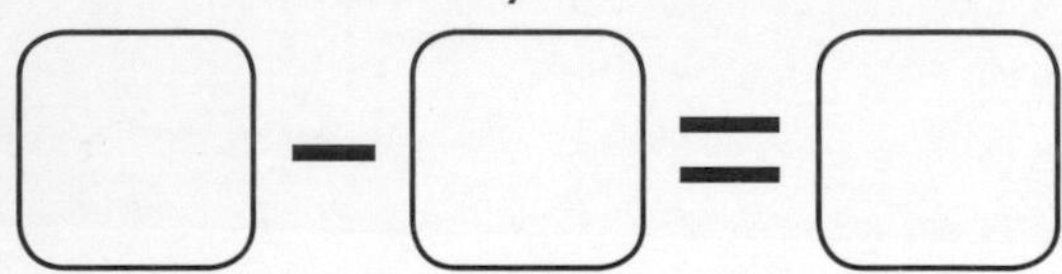

Caleb played the ring-the-bell game, scoring **100** points on his second try. He beat his first score by **37** points. How many points was his first score?

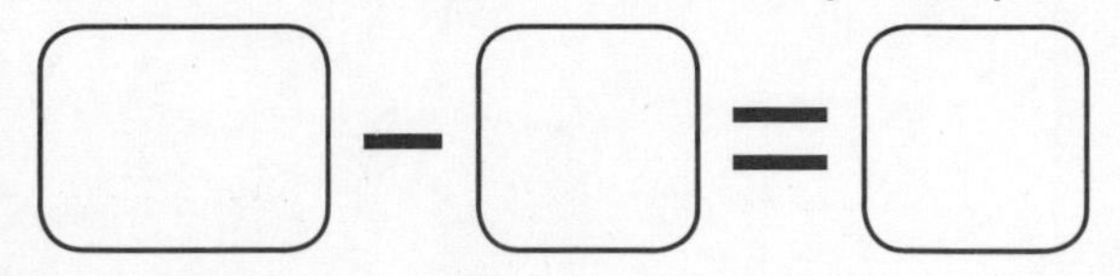

Julie and Anita both played the Milk Bottle game a few times. In all, Julie knocked down **4** fewer bottles than Anita did. Anita knocked down **21** bottles. How many bottles did Julie knock down?

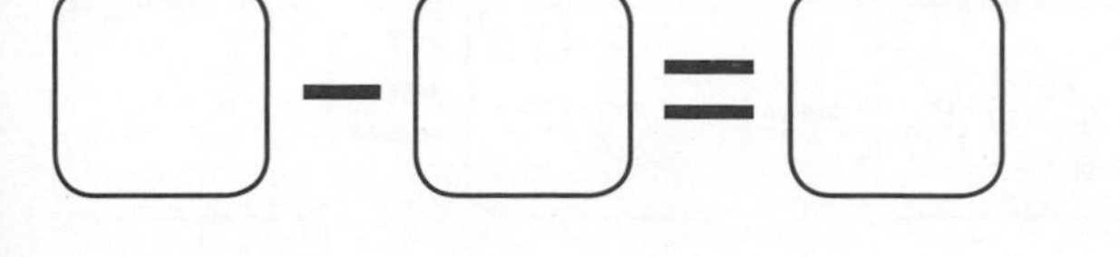

Tony made **82** pizza slices to feed the crowd. He sold **74** slices by the end of the day. How many pizza slices did Tony have left?

Can you find at least **20** differences between these scenes?

Triple Scoop

You can use place values to subtract three-digit numbers.

Here's the scoop: you can use many of the same strategies to subtract three-digit numbers as you use with two-digit numbers. One way is with base-ten drawings. Here's how.

Draw squares for hundreds, lines for tens, and dots for ones.

348 − 135 = ?

Cross off the number to be subtracted, by place value.

Then count the remaining hundreds, tens, and ones to find the answer.

348 − 135 = 213

Solve the equations. Draw to show your work.

465 − 314 = ☐

786 − 606 = ☐

579 − 247 = ☐

468 − 111 = ☐

$359 - 225 =$ ☐ $649 - 243 =$ ☐

$868 - 128 =$ ☐ $788 - 352 =$ ☐

$793 - 531 =$ ☐ $577 - 164 =$ ☐

Circle the **2** triple-scoop ice-cream cones that are the same.

Break It Open!

You can break open three-digit numbers to help you subtract. Here's how.

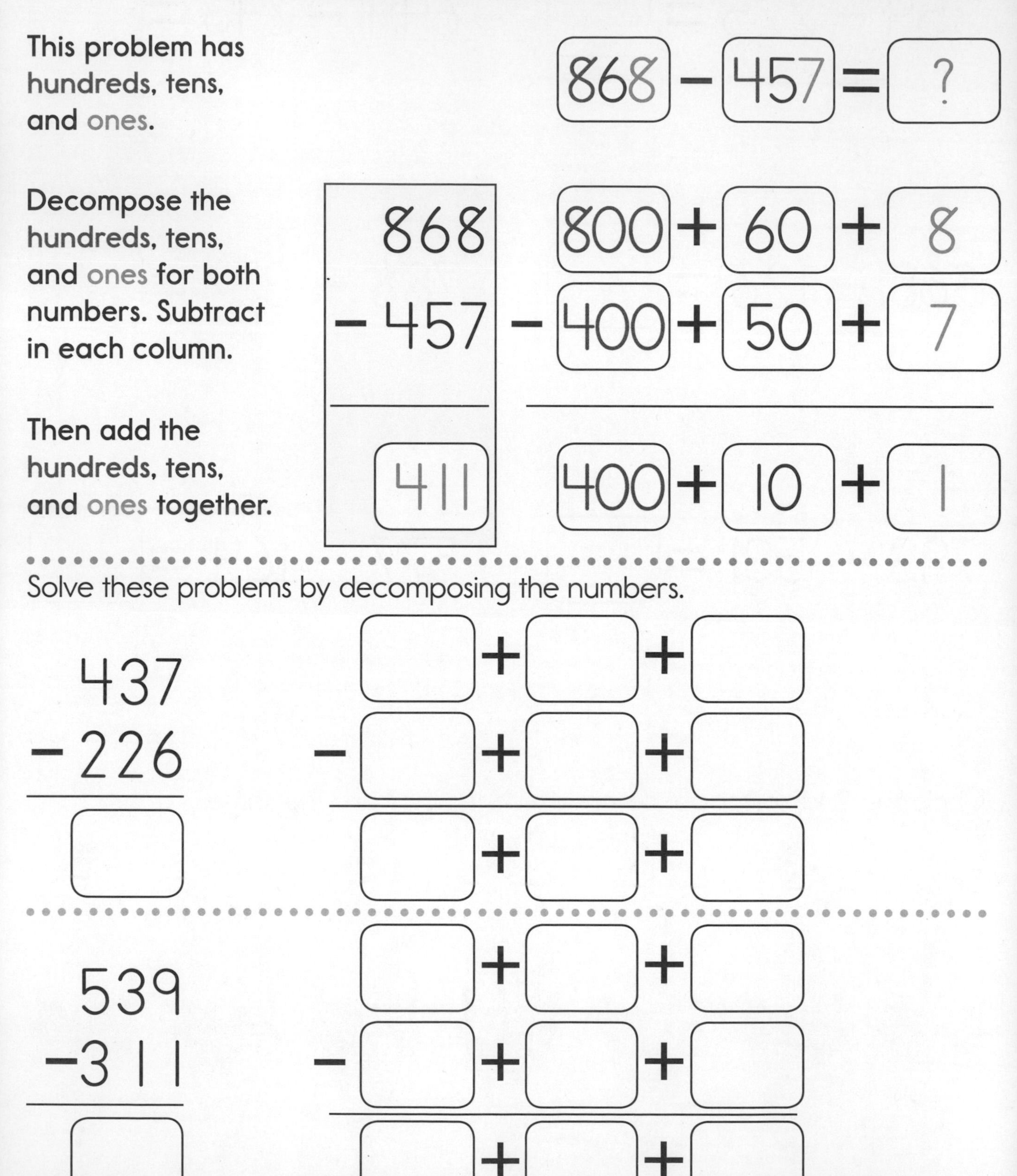

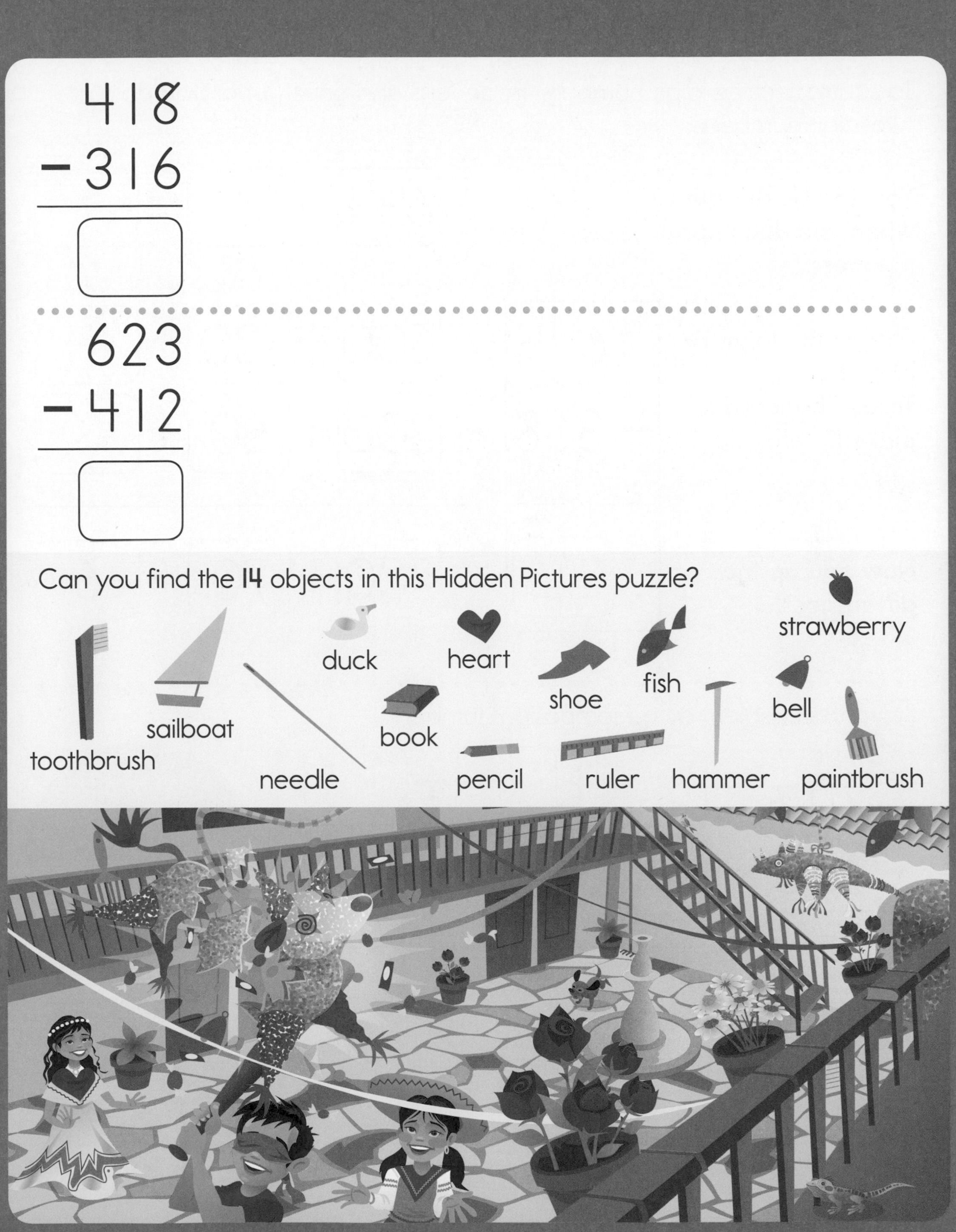
418
- 316
623
- 412
Can you find the 14 objects in this Hidden Pictures puzzle?
toothbrush
sailboat
needle
duck
book
heart
pencil
shoe
ruler
fish
hammer
bell
strawberry
paintbrush

Team Players

To subtract three-digit numbers, trade tens and ones just as you do for two-digit numbers.

You can be flexible when you decompose numbers.

644 − 368 = ?

Trade 1 ten to make 10 ones.
Trade 1 hundred to make 10 tens.

644		500	+	130	+	14
− 368	−	300	+	60	+	8
276		200	+	70	+	6

Now add up the differences.

Solve this problem by decomposing numbers.

747		☐	+	☐	+	☐
− 266	−	☐	+	☐	+	☐
☐		☐	+	☐	+	☐

What do you call a soccer player who loves subtraction?

A math-lete

Solve these subtraction problems. Remember to trade from the tens place when you need more ones, and to trade from the hundreds place when you need more tens.

$$\begin{array}{r} 153 \\ -\ 61 \\ \hline \square \end{array}$$

$$\begin{array}{r} 253 \\ -166 \\ \hline \square \end{array}$$

Each of these soccer players has something in common with the other **2** soccer players in the same row. For example, in the first row across all **3** players have a soccer ball. Look at the other rows across, down, and diagonally. Can you tell what's alike in each row?

The Power of Zero

What happens when a **0** appears in the ones or tens place of a three-digit number? It's a trade: **0** ones can become **10** ones, and **0** tens can become **10** tens.

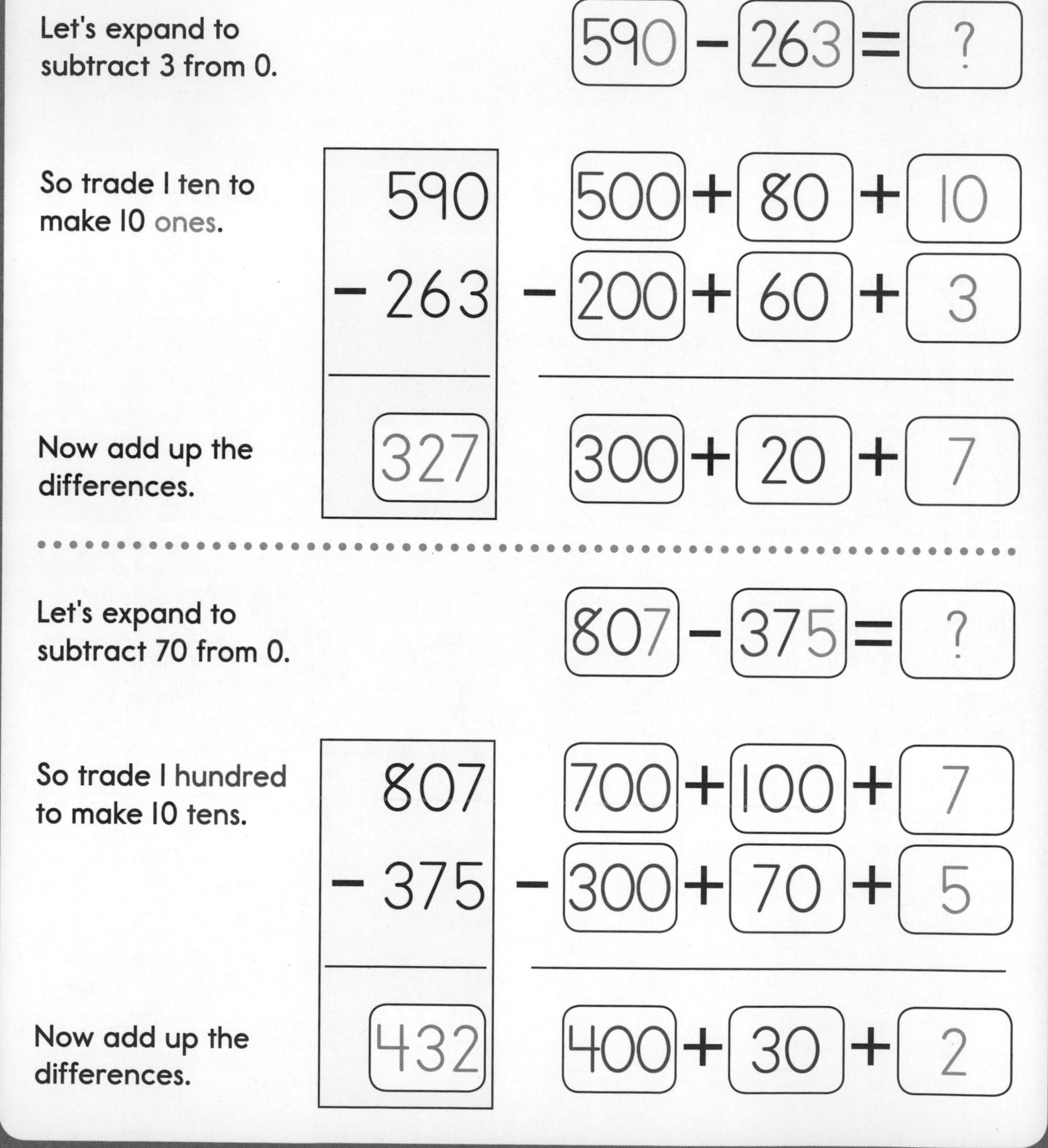

$170 - 34 = \square$

$906 - 543 = \square$

$507 - 263 = \square$

$209 - 118 = \square$

What did the plus sign say to the minus sign?

"You are so negative!"

Account Ants

It's harvest time! Solve these word problems to help the ants keep track of all the fruit, seeds, and nuts they have gathered. You can use any of the subtraction strategies you've learned.

Andrea and Ansel found **264** acorns today. Yesterday they found **142**. How many more acorns did they find today than yesterday?

Anika picked **452** blueberries. Andre picked **124** fewer blueberries than Anika. How many blueberries did Andre pick?

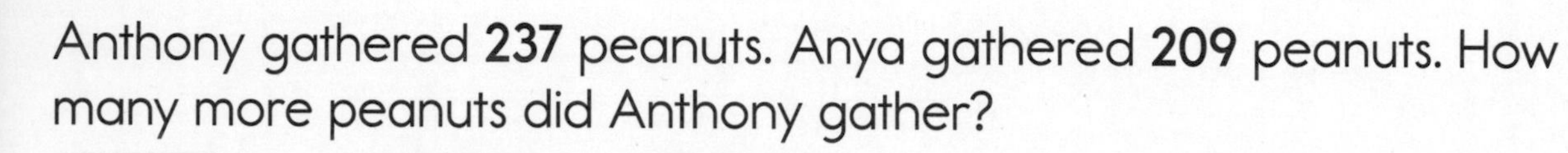

Anthony gathered **237** peanuts. Anya gathered **209** peanuts. How many more peanuts did Anthony gather?

Together Angela and Andrew picked **310** strawberries. Angela picked **166** of them. How many did Andrew pick?

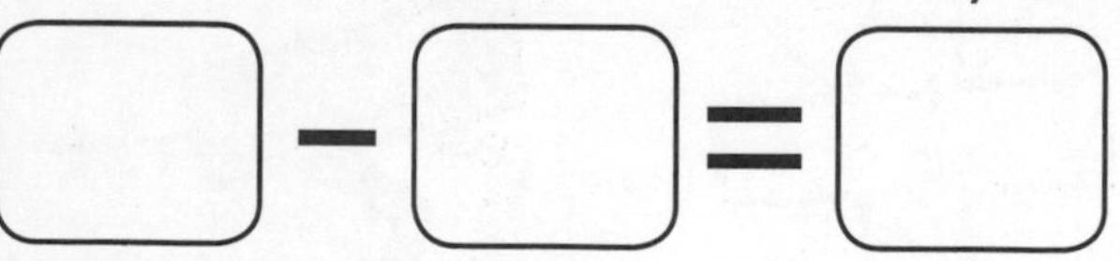

Antonia collected **643** seeds. But the wind blew **79** seeds away!
How many seeds did Antonia have left?

The buckets are filled with **889** strawberries and blueberries.
All but **392** are strawberries. How many are blueberries?

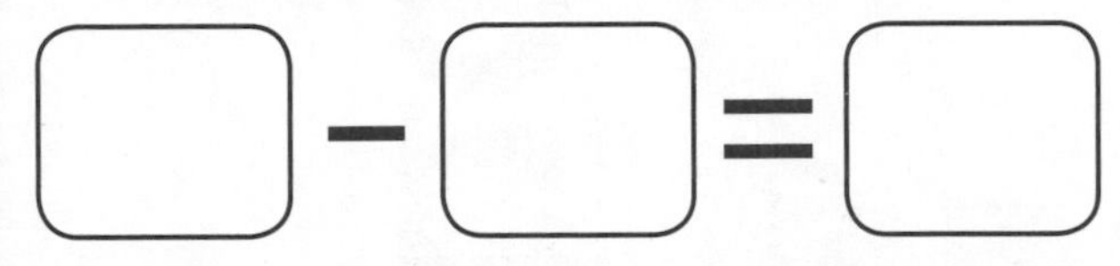

Find the **15** objects in this Hidden Pictures puzzle. Which of your answers matches the number on Mr. Hopper's calculator?

Highlights
SECOND GRADE
2
Congratulations!
(your name)
worked hard
and finished the
Subtraction
Learning Fun Workbook

Inside Front Cover

Why did the sun go to school?

TO GET BRIGHTER

Pages 2–3 Count Down!

10-4=6
9 8 7 6

11-4=7
10 9 8 7

13-3=10
12 11 10

12-6=6
11 10 9 8 7 6

18-6=12
17 16 15 14 13 12

7-4=3
17-2=15
8-2=6

16-3=13
9-3=6
11-5=6

Pages 4–5 Robot Parts

12 − 7 = 5 (12: 7, 5)
15 − 9 = 6 (15: 9, 6)
11 − 7 = 4 (11: 7, 4)
16 − 1 = 15 (16: 1, 15)

18 − 3 = 15 (18: 3, 15)
12 − 4 = 8 (12: 4, 8)
13 − 7 = 6 (13: 7, 6)
17 − 4 = 13 (17: 4, 13)
11 − 2 = 9 (11: 2, 9)
20 − 6 = 14 (20: 6, 14)

Pages 6–7 All in the Family

7-4=3
4+3=7

16-5=11
11+5=16

16-9=7
9+7=16

12-5=7
7+5=12

13-6=7
6+7=13

8-3=5
5+3=8

14-4=10
10+4=14

19-8=11
8+11=19

11-6=5
5+6=11

17-7=10
10+7=17

9-5=4
4+5=9

15-4=11
11+4=15

Pages 8–9 Jump on It!

9-1=8 7-6=1 14-0=14 8-2=6
13-7=6 15-5=10 10-7=3 17-12=5
10-2=8 13-10=3 20-3=17 13-6=7
20-4=16 14-6=8

Pages 10–11 In Its Place

37

Tens	Ones
3	7

91

Tens	Ones
9	1

318

Hundreds	Tens	Ones
3	1	8

117

Hundreds	Tens	Ones
1	1	7

14

Tens	Ones
1	4

52

Tens	Ones
5	2

854

Hundreds	Tens	Ones
8	5	4

499

Hundreds	Tens	Ones
4	9	9

	Larry	Lily	Leapy	1st	2nd	3rd
Lucas	X	O	X	X	X	O
Logan	X	X	O	O	X	X
Leah	O	X	X	X	O	X

Lucas: Lily, 3rd place
Logan: Leapy, 1st place
Leah: Larry, 2nd place

Pages 12–13 Ten Less, Anyone?

10 less than 254 is 244.
10 less than 167 is 157.
10 less than 498 is 488.
10 less than 777 is 767.
10 less than 652 is 642.
100 less than 221 is 121.
100 less than 302 is 202.
100 less than 543 is 443.
100 less than 633 is 533.
100 less than 806 is 706.

Pages 14–15 What's Next?

158 148 138 128 — 599 589 579 569
605 505 405 305 — 100 90 80 70
444 434 424 414 — 864 764 664 564
820 720 620 520 — 292 282 272 262

Pages 14–15
What's Next?

Pages 16–17
Cross It Off!

33-12=21
49-15=34
25-14=11
93-21=72

87-33=54
77-16=61
68-22=46
55-43=12

74-23=51
57-37=20
100-33=67
88-14=74

59-42=17
96-51=45
68-26=42
77-44=33

T 44	T 20	M 61	H 92	A 45
R 74	E 29	E 21	E 64	A 54
L 10	I 67	T 72	M 34	F 36
R 51	F 17	A 83	Y 46	B 57
E 71	J 42	K 12	T 57	H 11

THE ELF-ABET

Page 19
Hang On!

57-11=46
48-23=25
97-21=76
43-24=19
61-19=42
74-16=58
39-18=21

39-17=22
68-31=37
53-32=21
95-28=67
51-36=15
88-29=59
100-79=21

Pages 20–21
Ramp Up

47-34=13
80-26=54
77-45=32
65-27=38
77-18=59

52-11=41
39-17=22
58-23=35
92-52=40
61-17=44

Pages 22–23
Tool Time

75-50=25
21-11=10
38-27=11
78-35=43

55-38=17
36-19=17
51-25=26
72-38=34
63-48=15
23-17=6

42-29=13
66-30=36
51-46=5
83-37=46

94-69=25
82-22=60
70-43=27
99-26=73

Page 25
Bits and Pieces

51-6=45
98-9=89
82-3=79
42-4=38

Page 24
Bits and Pieces

46 - 8 = 38
5 3
46 - 5 = 41
41 - 3 = 38
46 - 8 = 38

25 - 7 = 18
4 3
25 - 4 = 21
21 - 3 = 18
25 - 7 = 18

Page 26
Break It Up!

32 - 21 = 11
30 - 20 = 10
2 - 1 = 1
10 + 1 = 11

88 - 37 = 51
80 - 30 = 50
8 - 7 = 1
50 + 1 = 51

Page 27
Break It Up!

77 - 22 = 55
70 - 20 = 50
7 - 2 = 5
50 + 5 = 55

59 - 35 = 24
50 - 30 = 20
9 - 5 = 4
20 + 4 = 24

Pages 28–29
Make a Trade!

24-7=17
27-9=18

46-7=39
53-5=48

43-8=35
62-5=57
41-9=32

96-7=89
53-7=46
92-6=86